A TEACHER'S
NIGHTMARE

From A Christian Perspective

ANTHONY DAYSE, PH.D.

ISBN: 978-1-965082-12-6

Publishing By: DemiCo National, LLC

www.DemiCoNational.com

Acknowledgements

To my beloved sisters, Dr. Sarah Dayse-Benson, Deborah Dayse Winston, Jeanetta Dayse-Garrett, and Juanda Collins, thank you for your unwavering love and support over the years. Your encouragement has been a source of strength throughout this journey.

To my brothers from another mother, Aziz Chabchab and Proctor F. Williams, I am deeply grateful for the brotherly love and companionship you have shown me.

Your friendship has been a constant blessing in my life.

-Anthony

TABLE OF CONTENTS

PREFACE

Teaching, often seen as a noble and rewarding profession, has its untold tales that unfold in the quiet corners of educators' minds. In "A Teacher's Nightmare," I delve into the anxieties, stresses, and challenges that educators face, reminding us all that teachers are not immune to human experience.

Embarking on this literary journey, we will confront the stark reality that the seemingly attractive and straightforward facade of teaching can be overshadowed by stressors that echo in the minds of teachers. Having navigated the educational landscape for over three decades, I've encountered and witnessed the nightmares that haunt educators – from the daunting prospect of being the new face in a school district to the disheartening feeling of not being favored by a principal.

Picture this: parents, driven by a fervent desire to secure unearned accolades for their children, riding the teacher's back with unwarranted demands. Add to the mix a deluge of meetings and an avalanche of demands throughout the school year, and the nightmare intensifies. It's a conundrum that leads many teachers to question, "To be or not to be?"

In "A Teacher's Nightmare," I unravel these threads of stress and uncertainty, offering not just a narrative but tangible strategies to navigate the storm. I pull back the curtain on the spiritual battles that often masquerade as mere professional challenges, reminding us that the true adversaries are not always flesh and blood but spiritual forces in high places.

Join me on this odyssey as we explore the remedies that provide resolution for the unfortunate events that plague the teaching profession. I advocate for letting God be the referee in this spiritual scrimmage, and together, we'll learn to don the armor that shields us against the unseen forces that attack us through others.

As we embark on this literary journey together, let the timeless melody of 'O Come, O Come, Emmanuel' echo in the corridors of our hearts. Just as the lyrics beckon for the presence of Emmanuel, meaning 'God with us,' may this book serve as a reminder that, in the midst of the challenges and joys of teaching, our calling is not solitary.

Let this be more than a book—it is an invitation to embrace teaching not as a mere survival expedition but as an enriching adventure. As we delve into the pages of 'A Teacher's Nightmare,' may the concept of salvation transform from a distant notion into a palpable reality for all who seek it through our Lord and Savior, Jesus Christ.

SECTION ONE

So, You're New at the District?

What led you to join this school district? It's a question that carries the weight of personal and professional significance, a decision woven into the fabric of your teaching journey.

In the intricate tapestry of educators' lives, the threads that draw us to a specific district are diverse. Some find themselves here due to the ebb and flow of life, uprooting and resettling in a new area, a fresh chapter waiting to be written. Others, freshly minted graduates, carry the torch of their alma mater, stepping into the hallowed halls where their educational roots lie.

There's a unique magic when familial ties intertwine with professional choices. For some, the decision is a familial legacy, a torch passed down through generations, where being an alumnus of the district becomes a cherished connection. Perhaps a family member or relative, a guiding light, beckons us to the corridors where they once trod, creating a familial bond within the educational community.

And then, there's the unspoken calling, the quiet whisper in the soul that says, 'This is where you're meant to be.' For those of us who hold a strong Christian belief, it's an acknowledgment that God's hand has orchestrated this alignment of time and place. It's a belief that we are not merely here by chance, but rather, divinely selected for a purpose that transcends the tangible aspects of teaching.

Certainly, one thing is clear – it's not for the pursuit of wealth. Teaching is a calling that resonates beyond financial aspirations, a journey marked by the currency of impact and inspiration rather than monetary gain.

So, as we embark on this exploration of the untold tales within the corridors of educators' minds, remember that the decision to join a school district is a tapestry of stories, a convergence of personal, professional, and divine threads that make each teacher's journey truly unique.

Specific expectations or Preconceived Notions

Before stepping into the embrace of this district, I, like any educator, carried with me a set of expectations and preconceived notions. There's an inherent anticipation when you become part of a new educational community, a mixture of excitement and curiosity about what lies ahead.

Expectations often linger in the air – perhaps the district is renowned for its commitment to innovation, a stronghold of academic excellence, or a nurturing environment for both students and educators. These expectations may have been woven into the tales shared by colleagues, whispered through the corridors of academia, or formed through the lens of public perception.

However, the beauty of joining a new district is the opportunity to infuse it with your unique creativity. It's a chance to bring your own color to the canvas, contributing to the vibrant tapestry of the educational landscape. Every teacher, with their distinct set of skills, experiences, and perspectives, becomes a brushstroke in the larger masterpiece.

Yet, spirituality plays a profound role in shaping and challenging these expectations. For those of us who believe that God orchestrates our paths, there's a recognition that our journey is guided by a higher purpose. It's an understanding that goes beyond mere sight or perception, urging us to play it by ear and embrace the unfolding narrative with faith.

Spirituality acts as a compass, navigating us through the realms of uncertainty and anchoring us in a belief that our presence in this district is not a mere coincidence. It's an intentional placement, a calling to contribute to the collective growth and development of both students and fellow educators.

As I reflect on those initial expectations, I am reminded that joining a district isn't just about what it can offer but what we, as teachers, can bring to its tapestry. It's a collaborative dance, a symphony where each note, influenced by personal expectations and divine guidance, contributes to the harmonious melody of education.

The Initial Impression

The first days in a new district are akin to stepping into uncharted territory, a journey that unfolds with a mix of excitement and trepidation. My own initiation into this unfamiliar landscape wasn't without its share of chaos, a reminder that even in the noble realm of teaching, the human experience is woven with threads of unpredictability.

As I navigated the corridors and classrooms of the district, each step seemed to introduce me to a new set of challenges – rules, regulations, and procedures that danced before my eyes like a complex choreography waiting to be mastered. The sheer volume of information, coupled with the pressure to assimilate quickly, threatened to create a whirlwind of overwhelm.

Yet, in the midst of this chaos, there was a reassuring presence. It was the understanding that, as educators, we're not alone in this journey. In those moments of uncertainty, a comforting whisper urged me to seek divine guidance. The Holy Spirit became a steadfast companion, a source of strength that allowed me to let go and let God take the lead.

I recall fervently asking for assistance, seeking divine intervention to help navigate the intricate maze of new faces, names, and protocols. It was a surrender to the belief that, even in the seemingly chaotic initiation, there was a divine plan unfolding.

This acknowledgment became a lifeline, transforming what could have been overwhelming days into an opportunity for spiritual growth and resilience. The chaos became a canvas on which faith painted a picture of trust and reliance on a higher power.

So, to those educators who find their first days in a new district unfolding into chaos, I say, fear not. Embrace the journey, seek divine guidance, and remember, even in the midst of chaos, there is a quiet assurance that God is nearby, ready to direct our paths in this new and unfamiliar environment.

Feelings About the District's Culture and
Environment

As I stepped into the heart of the district, its culture and environment unfolded before me like a tapestry of uncharted experiences. The initial observations were a blend of curiosity and trepidation, a reminder that every district has its unique identity waiting to be understood.

The culture of a district is like a symphony of traditions, unwritten rules, and collective behaviors that shape the educational landscape. It became evident early on that adapting to this cultural symphony was crucial for success. Yet, the question lingered: How do you synchronize your own style with the district's cultural melody?

In those early days, I discovered that success wasn't solely determined by how well one adapted to the district's culture. It was equally about forging connections – not just with colleagues but, more importantly, with God and those seasoned saints who understood the district's culture like second nature.

Imagine it as a dance, where your steps align not only with the cultural rhythm but also with the divine guidance that comes from connecting with the Holy Spirit. It became a delicate balance, a unique form of multi-tasking where learning the district's ways was accompanied by staying attuned to the whispers of the Holy Spirit.

I quickly realized that attempting to navigate the new environment solely through personal effort was a misconception. The key was not just in learning new ways but in seeking knowledge and protection simultaneously. This realization transformed my approach, bringing a sense of humility and openness to the process.

As educators, we sometimes fall into the trap of thinking we can do it all on our own. However, being in a new environment, learning new ways requires a different perspective. It's about acknowledging the power of connection – with the culture, with colleagues, and most importantly, with the divine presence that guides us through the unexplored terrain.

So, to educators stepping into a new district, I say: Embrace the cultural symphony, dance with the divine, and know that in connecting with both, you gain not just knowledge but a shield of protection in this intricate dance of adaptation.

Navigating the Unknown

As I stepped into the unknown territory of a new district, immediate challenges greeted me like unexpected guests, each demanding attention and swift navigation. It's often said that 'the devil is busy,' and indeed, being a newcomer felt like stepping onto a battlefield where the unexpected lurked around every corner.

The eagerness to fit in and excel in a new environment is a universal experience for any newcomer. The landscape of unfamiliar faces, procedures, and expectations can be overwhelming. Every step feels like deciphering a complex puzzle, and the pressure to find one's place intensifies.

In those initial days, the challenges were not abstract; they manifested as real-life scenarios that tested my adaptability and resilience. From decoding the unspoken norms of the staffroom to understanding the intricacies of administrative processes, each challenge seemed like a hurdle in the race to integration.

Amidst the chaos of chaotic beginnings, prayer emerged as a powerful tool that impacted every aspect of my journey. It became more than a routine; it was a lifeline, a source of guidance and strength in moments of confusion and uncertainty. The chaotic symphony of a newcomer's initiation found harmony through the spiritual practice of seeking divine intervention.

Navigating the challenges of being a newcomer is not just a logistical endeavor; it's a transformative journey that demands not only professional adaptability but a spiritual anchoring. The unexpected surprises, once seen as obstacles, became opportunities for growth and connection – a testament to the profound impact of prayer in reshaping a chaotic beginning.

So, to those who find themselves on the threshold of a new district, I say: Embrace the challenges, navigate with resilience, and let prayer be the compass that guides you through the intricate maze of being a newcomer. In the chaos, discover the potential for growth, and witness how the journey transforms from a daunting nightmare into a purposeful adventure.

Understanding the Dynamics of the District

Embarking on the journey of getting to know my colleagues and unraveling the intricate dynamics of the district was akin to navigating a labyrinth of relationships and unwritten rules. The seemingly simple task of connection held layers of complexity that required more than just a casual smile or small talk.

In the realm of education, where collaboration is key, the process of forming meaningful connections with colleagues can be both a daunting challenge and a rewarding endeavor. As a newcomer, I quickly realized that the chess game of life required strategic moves to understand and be understood.

My approach transformed when I discovered the power of prayer as a guiding force in this delicate dance of getting to know others. Instead of relying solely on small talk or forced conversations, I began my days with a prayer, seeking divine intervention to bring willing and supportive colleagues into my path. It was a shift from merely engaging in social niceties to purposefully connecting with those who would contribute positively to my calling as an educator.

The dynamics of a district, like the ebb and flow of a chess game, revealed themselves gradually. Each colleague became a piece on the board, and understanding their unique moves and strategies became essential. What seemed like a challenge transformed into an opportunity for growth and collaboration.

Through prayer, I not only found willing colleagues but also gained insights into the unspoken norms and intricacies of the district. The chess game of life became a collective effort, with each move guided by a higher purpose. The connection with colleagues wasn't just a formality; it became a shared journey of navigating the complexities of education.

To those stepping into a new district, I offer this lesson from my own experience: Approach the task of getting to know your colleagues not as a mere social exercise but as a spiritual journey. Let prayer be your compass, guiding you to the individuals who will enrich your calling and contribute to the collective success of the district. In the game of life, where each move matters, a prayerful approach can transform the dynamics and make the journey more meaningful.

Building Relationships

Embarking on the journey of establishing connections with fellow educators, staff, and administrators has been nothing short of a transformative experience. In the tapestry of my teaching career, these connections have woven threads of support, understanding, and shared purpose.

Every school year, as I stood on the precipice of a new beginning, I found solace and strength in a simple yet powerful ritual – prayer. Before the hustle and bustle of the school day commenced, I would take a moment to seek divine guidance and protection. Little did I know that this prayer would set the stage for meaningful connections that would shape my professional journey.

One vivid memory takes me back to a challenging year when I felt like a chess piece navigating an unfamiliar board. Through prayer, I found the assurance that God would strategically place the right players in my path. And indeed, as the school year unfolded, I encountered fellow educators, staff, and administrators who became invaluable allies.

In the realm of education, where collaboration is the heartbeat of success, the connections we forge with those around us carry profound significance. My belief in the reciprocity of energy and intentionality guided my approach to these connections. What I put into the professional space was returned to me in the form of support, camaraderie, and shared wisdom.

There were moments of shared laughter in the teacher's lounge, collaborative planning sessions that birthed innovative ideas, and the reassurance of knowing that, as educators, we were not solitary warriors but a collective force striving for the betterment of our students.

The impact of these connections extended beyond the professional realm. They became the pillars that supported me during challenging times, the beacons of light during moments of uncertainty, and the shared triumphs that made the journey worthwhile.

As I reflect on the mosaic of connections that have adorned my teaching career, I am reminded that teaching is not merely a profession; it is a community of dedicated individuals united by a common purpose. Through prayer and intentional efforts, I have had the privilege of establishing connections that have not only enhanced my teaching experience but have also made the quiet corners of educators' minds a place of shared understanding and support.

Mentorship Programs or Support Systems?

Reflecting on my journey as a teacher, the question of mentorship programs and support systems for new teachers evokes a nuanced response. Yes, there are mentorship programs, but the landscape has evolved, and the dynamics have shifted in ways that demand our attention.

In the bygone era, mentorship was akin to a guiding hand, a steady presence that helped navigate the intricate tapestry of teaching. However, the contemporary educational milieu presents a different picture. Mentorship programs still exist, but the demands on educators have reached unprecedented heights.

As a new teacher, I yearned for the camaraderie and wisdom that a mentor could offer. The reality, however, was that everyone, seasoned educators included, found themselves entangled in the web of overwhelming responsibilities. Mentorship became a casualty of the teacher shortage crisis, where the weight of additional demands eclipsed the time once dedicated to guiding the next generation of educators.

The mentorship landscape transformed into a challenging terrain, where the desire to help was overshadowed by the sheer magnitude of responsibilities. The teacher shortage not only created a void in staffing but also cast a shadow on the mentorship opportunities that were once readily available.

The scarcity of mentors doesn't stem from a lack of willingness but rather from the systemic challenges that have permeated the educational sphere. Teachers, burdened by heavier workloads and broader responsibilities, grapple with finding the time and resources to engage in mentorship as they once did.

This shift in mentorship dynamics is not an isolated phenomenon; it mirrors the broader changes in our society. The external pressures and challenges that have infiltrated our schools reflect a manifestation of the evolving world around us. As Christian teachers, we are called to be vigilant, as these challenges contribute to a narrative that echoes the warnings of the last days.

Despite the challenges, there remains a collective desire to nurture the next generation of educators. The limitations in mentorship programs are not a testament to a lack of dedication but rather a plea for systemic changes that recognize and address the multifaceted challenges facing our educational institutions.

As we navigate this landscape, it becomes imperative for Christian teachers to discern the signs of the times, seeking wisdom and guidance from above. In the face of evolving challenges, we are reminded that our calling as educators extends beyond the classroom, encompassing a commitment to shaping the future in a world that is in constant flux.

Challenges Faced

As I reflect on the challenges encountered as a newcomer to the district, one particular hurdle stands out vividly – the daunting reality of assignments designed for one teacher but grounded in the workload of two. Picture this: classrooms filled to the brim, not due to an abundance of teachers, but rather scarcity. The echoes of a teacher shortage reverberate through the hallways, and the impact on both performance and morale is palpable.

The unique challenge faced by new teachers is not merely about adapting to a different environment but grappling with a workload that seems insurmountable.

The strain on resources has resulted in assignments that stretch the limits of one individual, pushing them beyond what is reasonable. This situation is not a testament to a lack of dedication or capability but rather a consequence of systemic challenges that transcend the individual.

Consider the high-spirited educator, driven by a passion for teaching and a desire to make a positive impact. Entering a district with enthusiasm and hope, only to be confronted with assignments that demand the workload of two, can be disheartening and spirit-breaking. The discouragement that sets in when faced with these specific hurdles is a shared experience among many newcomers.

The impact on teacher morale becomes a critical concern. As educators, we thrive on the ability to inspire and uplift our students. However, when faced with challenges that hinder our own enthusiasm and well-being, the ripple effect extends beyond the individual. It touches the very fabric of the teaching environment, casting shadows on the potential for a positive and nurturing learning space.

The challenges unique to being new to the district go beyond mere adjustments to a different educational landscape. They penetrate the core of our commitment to education and reveal the need for systemic changes. This is not a plea for sympathy but a call to recognize the strains within the profession and work collectively to address them.

As we navigate these hurdles, it becomes imperative for both new and experienced educators to unite in advocating for changes that foster a supportive and sustainable teaching environment. Let this challenge be a rallying cry for systemic improvements that ensure every teacher, new or seasoned, can fulfill their noble calling without the weight of undue burdens.

Challenges Contribute to Anxieties and Stresses

The challenges inherent in the teaching profession are not just professional hurdles; they are silent architects of anxieties and stresses that find their dwelling in the quiet corners of educators' minds. As I reflect on the experiences shared in the book's preface, it becomes evident that these challenges, left unaddressed, morph into burdens that weigh heavily on the shoulders of teachers.

Imagine navigating a landscape where demands seem incessant, expectations loom large, and the weight of responsibilities threatens to overwhelm. In such an environment, anxieties and stresses find fertile ground to take root. The constant juggling act required in teaching, combined with external pressures, contributes to sleepless nights and a pervasive sense of worry.

Anxieties and stresses develop when there are no outlets for release, no avenues to let go and let God step in. The profession's demands can create a relentless cycle, leaving educators feeling trapped in a web of challenges without a lifeline. It's a scenario that many teachers can resonate with, a silent struggle that often goes unnoticed.

In my journey, I've learned the transformative power of incorporating faith into the fabric of daily living. 'God does not want us to worry about nothing but pray about everything,' a mantra that has become my refuge in the face of mounting challenges. Letting go and allowing God to take the reins becomes not just a spiritual practice but a practical strategy for navigating the storms within the teaching profession.

I recall nights when the weight of responsibilities threatened to overshadow the joy of teaching. It was in those moments that I turned to prayer, seeking solace and guidance from a higher power. The result was a profound shift in perspective, a reminder that the journey of a teacher is not meant to be born alone.

This revelation forms the essence of the book, as it unravels the untold tales of anxieties and stresses faced by educators. It is a call to recognize the humanity within the teaching profession, to acknowledge the silent struggles that shape the experiences of every teacher. As we delve into these pages, we may find not just a narrative but a shared understanding that, through faith, we can confront the challenges and emerge stronger, resilient, and ready to transform our calling into an enriching and fulfilling adventure.

Parental Interactions

.

In the intricate tapestry of teaching, early interactions with parents become pivotal moments that shape the dynamics of the entire school year. These encounters are not mere transactions but opportunities to set the tone for collaboration and understanding. As I reflect on my own journey, I am reminded of the profound influence that a spiritual connection can have on these interactions.

Picture this: the anticipation of meeting parents for the first time, each carrying a unique set of expectations and hopes for their child's academic journey. In these moments, how you are perceived by others becomes a crucial factor in laying the foundation for meaningful partnerships.

Having a spiritual connection goes beyond religious affiliation; it manifests in the way we speak, respond to challenges, and navigate the complexities of the teaching profession. It's a glow that emanates from within, a divine shine that becomes unmistakable in our interactions.

One early interaction that stands out in my memory is a parent-teacher meeting where a challenging situation arose. A student was facing academic struggles, and the parent, understandably concerned, approached the meeting with a mix of apprehension and hope. In that moment, my spiritual connection guided my responses. Instead of focusing solely on the academic challenges, I acknowledged the unique strengths and potential of the student, offering a perspective rooted in positivity and encouragement.

The result was transformative. The parents, initially anxious, left the meeting with a sense of reassurance and gratitude. This encounter set the stage for a collaborative relationship, demonstrating the power of a spiritual connection in shaping perceptions and fostering understanding.

These early interactions, infused with the divine glow of spiritual connection, become opportunities to build bridges of trust and empathy. Parents, attuned to the authenticity that comes with spiritual grounding, are more likely to see beyond the surface and recognize the genuine commitment to their child's well-being.

In the pages of 'A Teacher's Nightmare,' I delve into the intricacies of such interactions, exploring how spirituality can be a guiding light in navigating the delicate balance of teacher-parent relationships. It's a reminder that, as educators, our influence extends beyond the classroom, reaching into the homes and hearts of the families we serve. Through the lens of spiritual connection, early interactions with parents become not just challenges but opportunities to illuminate the path toward a collaborative and enriching educational journey.

Balancing Professional and Personal Life

The demands of a new role in the realm of teaching create a ripple effect that extends beyond the classroom, seeping into the quiet corners of one's personal life. As I reflect on the challenges that accompany a shift in responsibilities, it becomes apparent that the ability to maintain a harmonious work-life balance is not just a skill; it's a testament to the foundation upon which you build your life.

Picture this: a Christian teacher stepping into a new role, facing a torrent of responsibilities that threaten to tip the delicate scales of work-life equilibrium. It's a scenario familiar to many educators, a juncture where the demands of the profession collide with the sanctuary of personal time.

In my journey, I've encountered moments when the demands seemed insurmountable, threatening to overshadow the tranquility of life outside work. However, the pivotal factor that transformed these challenges into manageable feats was the unwavering presence of Christ at the center of my life.

The Christian teacher, anchored in faith, views the demands of the new role from a different vantage point. What may appear as an overwhelming workload becomes an opportunity to showcase resilience and steadfastness. It's a mindset shift that allows you to rebuke the negative hands dealt by professional challenges and withstand the storms with unwavering resolve.

Consider a scenario where the demands of lesson planning, grading, and administrative tasks pile up, encroaching on personal time. Instead of succumbing to the pressure, a Christian teacher draws strength from their spiritual foundation. They prioritize prayer, seeking guidance and divine intervention in managing time effectively. This intentional act of surrendering the burdens to Christ transforms the daunting demands into manageable responsibilities.

Moreover, the Christian teacher embraces the concept of 'Sabbath rest' not just as a religious observance but as a practical strategy for maintaining work-life balance. This intentional rest, grounded in faith, becomes a sanctuary for rejuvenation, allowing the teacher to return to their professional responsibilities with a refreshed spirit.

As you continue to embark on this literary journey, discover the transformative power of infusing your professional life with the principles of faith, turning the demands of a new role into steppingstones toward a harmonious and fulfilling work-life balance.

Personal and Professional
Stressors Intertwined?

Have you ever felt the gravitational pull of personal and professional stressors intertwining, creating a web that seems impossible to navigate? It's a scenario familiar to many educators, a juncture where the demands of personal life weave into the fabric of professional responsibilities.

In the intricate dance between personal and professional realms, the key lies in realizing that our personal lives must involve a guiding force that extends its influence into our professional journey. As educators, we must acknowledge that we are called to a work that intricately intertwines and demands a delicate balance.

Picture this: a teacher juggling the demands of lesson planning, grading, and administrative tasks while simultaneously dealing with personal challenges – be it familial, health-related, or emotional. It's a delicate balancing act that, if not approached with intentionality, can tip the scales toward overwhelming stress.

The crux of the matter is understanding that our personal and professional lives are not isolated entities but interconnected threads in the tapestry of our existence. This realization becomes even more profound when we recognize that, as educators, we are called by a higher force – a divine purpose that shapes our work.

The intertwining of personal and professional stressors serves as a gentle reminder that seeking balance is not just a professional skill; it's a spiritual pursuit. In those moments when the threads threaten to tangle, we must hold on to God's unchanging hands, anchoring ourselves in the unwavering strength that transcends the temporal challenges we face.

Consider a scenario where personal challenges, such as health issues or family concerns, vie for attention amidst the relentless demands of the teaching profession. In these moments, the intertwining stressors become a call to action – a call to seek guidance, solace, and balance from the divine source that called us to this noble work.

As we navigate the delicate balance between personal and professional realms, let us keep in mind the sacred calling that binds the two. Holding on to God's unchanging hands becomes not just a poetic phrase but a tangible strategy for weathering the storms that arise when the threads of personal and professional stressors intertwine.

In the pages of our teaching journey, let us explore the profound truth that acknowledging the intertwining nature of personal and professional stressors is the first step toward achieving balance. It's an exploration of how, by holding on to God's unchanging hands, we can navigate the intricate dance of our calling with resilience, faith, and a deep sense of purpose.

Strategies for Coping

As a newcomer navigating the uncertainties and stresses of a new teaching role, I discovered the power of embracing spiritual coping mechanisms that not only provided solace but became guiding lights in my journey.

Picture this: stepping into a new school district, unfamiliar faces, and the weight of professional expectations. It's a scenario that can be overwhelming, and in those moments, I found solace in joining a prayer circle. This intentional act of seeking spiritual support became a cornerstone of my coping mechanism.

Attending mid-week Bible studies emerged as a sanctuary amidst the demands of the school week. These gatherings offered a sacred space to rejuvenate my spirit, gain insights from fellow believers, and find resonance in the teachings that transcended the challenges I faced as a newcomer.

Connecting with other Christian teachers became more than a support network; it was a lifeline. Sharing experiences, offering prayers for one another, and standing united in our faith created a sense of camaraderie that eased the burden of uncertainties. It was a reminder that, as teachers, we are not alone in our journey.

Regularly immersing myself in the teachings of the Bible became more than a religious practice; it was a source of wisdom and guidance. The scriptures became a manual for navigating the complexities of the education landscape. Searching for similarities in the Bible to gain knowledge of how to handle specific situations became a practical tool in my toolkit.

But beyond the tangible coping mechanisms, there was a profound realization – the assurance that 'no weapon formed against me shall prosper.' This biblical truth became an anchor in moments when challenges seemed insurmountable. It's a declaration of resilience, a reminder that the spiritual fortification we build through prayer, study, and fellowship acts as a shield against the adversities that may arise.

In the intricate dance between the spiritual and the professional, these coping mechanisms weren't just rituals; they were transformative practices that shaped my resilience, clarity of purpose, and sense of belonging in the teaching community.

So, to my fellow educators navigating the unpredictable terrain of a new teaching role, consider embracing these spiritual coping mechanisms. They are not just rituals; they are powerful tools that can turn uncertainties into opportunities for growth, stress into strength, and challenges into triumphs. As we put on our full armor, fortified by prayer, study, and fellowship, we not only withstand the storms but emerge stronger and more resilient in our calling as educators.

Lessons Learned

As I reflect on the pivotal lessons learned during my initial days at the district, the essence of putting God first emerges as the guiding principle that shaped my journey.

Stepping into a new district, I encountered a myriad of challenges, each demanding a unique response. In those moments of uncertainty, I learned that the anchor of my resilience and the compass for my decisions must be grounded in a faith-driven approach.

Picture the first days, the maze of new faces, unfamiliar procedures, and the weight of expectations.

It's a scenario that can be daunting, but the resounding lesson was clear – put God first. This wasn't merely a passive acknowledgment; it was an intentional act of seeking divine guidance, protection, and support.

Amidst the whirlwind of administrative intricacies and the demands of a new educational landscape, the act of keeping God included became more than a ritual; it became a source of strength. There were moments when challenges seemed insurmountable, but through prayer and a continuous request for the Holy Spirit's guidance, I found clarity and resilience.

One specific instance stands out, a situation where decisions needed to be made swiftly, and the path forward was unclear. In those moments, the lessons learned in putting God first became a practical tool for discernment. Seeking divine wisdom in the face of ambiguity led to a resolution that surpassed my own understanding.

As I navigated the complexities of being new to the district, the lessons learned weren't confined to procedural knowledge or administrative acumen. They extended into the realm of spiritual fortitude, reminding me that seeking God's guidance isn't just a one-time act but a continuous practice.

So, to those embarking on their journey in a new district, consider this reflection not just as a piece of advice but as a testament to the transformative power of prioritizing your faith. In the tapestry of challenges, uncertainties, and victories that characterize the teaching profession, let the lesson of putting God first be the thread that weaves resilience, clarity, and divine guidance into the fabric of your journey.

Looking Ahead

As I navigated the uncharted waters of acclimating to a new district, my aspirations and goals were intricately woven into the fabric of my calling as an educator. It wasn't just about adapting to a new administrative landscape; it was about fulfilling the purpose that God had called me to.

In those initial days, amid the whirlwind of new faces and unfamiliar procedures, I set a profound goal for myself – to be the beacon of light in every classroom I entered. This wasn't a mere professional aspiration; it was a spiritual commitment to make a lasting difference in the lives of the young minds entrusted to my care.

One specific instance stands out vividly. It was a moment when the challenges of acclimating seemed overwhelming, and doubt began to cast its shadow. In that moment of vulnerability, my goal became a source of strength. I reminded myself that I wasn't just there to navigate administrative intricacies; I was there to be the sun that shines in the lives of my students.

The goal was simple yet profound – to do what God had called me to do. It was a daily reminder that my role transcended the conventional boundaries of education; it was a divine mission to impact a child's life positively.

As I reflect on those early aspirations, I realize that the goal wasn't just about professional excellence; it was about creating an environment where students felt the warmth of encouragement, the illumination of knowledge, and the nurturing embrace of a caring teacher.

So, to educators stepping into new districts, let your aspirations be more than just checkboxes on a career to-do list. Let them be a reflection of your divine calling, a commitment to be the sunlight that dispels darkness, ignites curiosity, and fosters a love for learning in every classroom you enter."

Notes

_____

_____

_____

_____

_____

_____

_____

_____

_____

_____

_____

_____

_____

_____

_____

_____

_____

_____

_____

_____

_____

_____

_____

A Teacher's Prayer for Being New at the District

Heavenly Father,

As I embark on this new journey in an unfamiliar district, I humbly seek Your guidance and wisdom. Open my heart and mind to absorb the new rules and procedures that govern this educational landscape. Surround me with supportive individuals who will not only guide me through the intricacies but also inspire my growth as an educator.

Lord, I place my trust in You to lead me to the right people, mentors, and resources that will contribute to my success in fulfilling the purpose for which You've called me to this place. Shield me from any uncertainties and challenges that may arise, allowing me to focus on the calling You've bestowed upon me.

Grant me the strength and resilience to adapt to this new environment and empower me to make a positive impact on the lives of the students I will serve. May Your divine presence be a constant source of reassurance and inspiration as I navigate through this chapter of my teaching career. In Your name, I pray. Amen.

Scriptures When We Need Them the Most

These scriptures emphasize the themes of trust, fearlessness, God's plans for our future, the guidance of His word, and the importance of committing one's ways to Him. They can offer solace and inspiration as teachers navigate the challenges and uncertainties of a new environment.

Isaiah 41:10 (NIV): Trust in the Lord with all your heart and lean not on your own understanding; in all your ways submit to him, and he will make your paths straight.

Jeremiah 29:11 (NIV): For I know the plans I have for you, declares the Lord, plans for welfare and not for evil, to give you a future and a hope.

Psalm 119:105 (NIV): Your word is a lamp for my feet, a light on my path.

Proverbs 16:3 (NIV): Commit to the Lord whatever you do, and he will establish your plans.

SECTION TWO

The Principal Don't Like Me

Christian faith guiding your approach to a favorable opinion

"When confronted with the sense that the principal may not view you favorably as a teacher, it's crucial to anchor yourself in the unwavering foundation of your Christian faith. Picture this scenario as a chapter in your life's narrative, where the principal's perspective is just one subplot in the grander story written by the Almighty.

Consider the narrative of Daniel in the lion's den. Like Daniel, your dedication to your calling as a teacher is witnessed and celebrated by a higher authority. If the principal's opinion seems unfavorable, remember that God's endorsement outweighs any human judgment.

I recall a specific instance in my career when misunderstandings with a principal arose. Instead of succumbing to panic, I chose to lean into my faith. I took inspiration from the biblical injunction, 'Do not be anxious about anything, but in every situation, by prayer and petition, with thanksgiving, present your requests to God.' (Philippians 4:6, NIV).

In those moments, I embraced a spirit of calm assurance, understanding that my true calling transcended any singular professional relationship. My approach was to actively seek divine intervention through prayer and reflection, trusting that God's guidance would illuminate the path forward.

In essence, my message is this: the opinion of one individual does not define your worth or purpose. In the intricate tapestry of your teaching journey, God's plan unfolds, and every perceived setback is an opportunity for divine intervention. So, when faced with the challenge of a less-than-favorable perception, look to your faith as the compass that steadies your course and allows you to navigate with resilience and grace.

Turning to Your Faith as
a Source of Strength and Guidance

In the intricate dance of our teaching journey, the chapter titled 'The Principal Don't Like Me' unveils a narrative that many educators may find familiar. When faced with conflicts or challenges in our professional sphere, especially with school leadership, how can Christian educators fortify themselves with the unyielding strength of their faith?

Think of this situation as a storm that can either shake the foundations or serve as a testament to the resilience of your convictions. The Psalmist's words, 'I lift up my eyes to the hills. From where does my help come? My help comes from the Lord, who made heaven and earth.' (Psalm 121:1-2, ESV), offer a profound reminder that, in times of turbulence, our ultimate source of strength transcends the human realm.

Allow me to share a personal reflection from my own journey. There was a time when conflicts with school leadership seemed insurmountable. Instead of succumbing to despair, I turned to prayer and sought solace in the wisdom of the Scriptures. Proverbs 3:5-6 became my anchor: 'Trust in the Lord with all your heart and lean not on your own understanding; in all your ways submit to him, and he will make your paths straight' (NIV). This became my guiding principle, a beacon of light amidst the storm.

Christian educators, in such moments, can turn to prayer, seeking divine guidance and surrendering their concerns to the higher purpose they serve. Embrace the strength found in unity with fellow believers; share your burdens and let the collective faith of your community uplift you. Remember that, just as in the biblical narrative of Daniel facing adversity, our faith can transform conflicts into opportunities for divine intervention.

So, when confronted with perceived conflicts, let your faith be the compass that not only guides but transforms the narrative. Embrace the assurance that your journey, even in challenging chapters, aligns with a divine plan, and through faith, you can find strength, wisdom, and the resilience to weather any storm.

Applying Biblical Principles

When faced with interpersonal challenges within the school environment, especially in the context of a strained relationship with the principal, the wisdom embedded in biblical principles becomes our guiding light.

Consider the analogy of putting on the full armor of God, as Ephesians 6:11 encourages us: 'Put on the whole armor of God, that you may be able to stand against the schemes of the devil' (ESV). This metaphorical armor, consisting of truth, righteousness, the gospel of peace, faith, salvation, and the word of God, is not just a picturesque concept but a practical strategy for navigating challenging relationships.

Let me delve deeper into this metaphor. Just as a soldier equips themselves with armor to face adversities on the battlefield, we, too, can arm ourselves with truth, maintaining integrity in our actions and communication. The breastplate of righteousness becomes our shield, guarding our hearts against bitterness and resentment. The gospel of peace leads us to seek reconciliation, fostering an environment of understanding.

Faith, akin to a helmet, protects our minds from doubt and discouragement, reminding us of our divine calling in the face of interpersonal strife. Salvation, a steadfast anchor, grounds us in the assurance that our ultimate allegiance lies with a higher purpose.

Drawing inspiration from biblical stories, consider the narrative of Joseph in Genesis. Despite facing betrayal and adversity, Joseph maintained his faith and integrity, ultimately emerging as a guiding force in Egypt. Likewise, we, as educators, can find strength in our faith and navigate strained relationships with grace and resilience.

So, when interpersonal challenges arise, let the biblical principles of armor guide your approach. Embrace the timeless wisdom woven into these narratives, transforming challenges into opportunities for growth, understanding, and ultimately, the triumph of faith.

Christian Teachers Can Maintain a Positive and
Christ-Like Attitude

In the crucible of challenges, particularly when Christian teachers perceive a lack of support or understanding from school leadership, maintaining a positive and Christ-like attitude becomes a profound testimony of faith. The path to resilience and grace is paved with intentional actions and steadfast principles.

One powerful strategy is to anchor oneself in prayer. When faced with adversity, seeking solace in communion with God provides not only spiritual strength but also a sense of guidance and purpose. The Psalms, in particular, offer a rich source of comfort and inspiration.

Additionally, cultivating a spirit of gratitude can be transformative. Despite the hurdles, consciously reflecting on the blessings and positive aspects of the teaching profession redirects focus and fosters an attitude of thanksgiving. This aligns with the biblical injunction to 'give thanks in all circumstances' (1 Thessalonians 5:18).

Practicing forgiveness is another Christ-like attribute that can permeate the atmosphere of adversity. By letting go of resentment and choosing to forgive, Christian teachers emulate the unconditional forgiveness modeled by Christ on the cross.

Engaging in Christian fellowship within the school community can create a supportive network. Connecting with like-minded colleagues for prayer meetings, Bible studies, or simply for mutual encouragement can uplift spirits and reinforce a sense of community.

Finally, adopting a servant-leadership mindset allows Christian teachers to emulate Christ's humility. By serving others selflessly, even in the face of adversity, they embody the transformative power of love and compassion.

So, when adversity knocks, Christian teachers are equipped not only with prayer but with a repertoire of Christ-like attitudes – gratitude, forgiveness, community, and servant leadership. In these intentional actions, the radiance of Christ's love can shine brightly, dispelling the shadows of adversity.

Prayers, Scriptures, or Spiritual Practices Can Be Incorporated Daily

There are specific prayers, scriptures, or spiritual practices that Christian educators can incorporate into their daily routine to navigate professional challenges and interpersonal conflicts within the school. Christian educators can fortify themselves daily by weaving specific prayers, scriptures, and spiritual practices into their routine. These intentional actions serve as a spiritual compass, guiding educators through the complexities of professional challenges and interpersonal conflicts within the school.

The Morning Prayer for Guidance: Begin each day with a prayer seeking divine guidance. Acknowledge the challenges ahead and invite God's wisdom to navigate through them. A simple yet powerful prayer can set a positive tone for the day.

Scripture Meditation – Philippians 4:13: In moments of self-doubt or when faced with seemingly insurmountable challenges, meditating on Philippians

4:13 ('I can do all things through Christ who strengthens me') can infuse educators with renewed strength and confidence.

Prayer of Forgiveness

Conflict can be inevitable, but incorporating a daily prayer of forgiveness is transformative. Ask for the grace to forgive others and seek forgiveness for any perceived wrongs. This practice aligns with the Lord's Prayer, emphasizing forgiveness as a cornerstone of Christian living.

Gratitude Journaling: Devote time to jot down daily expressions of gratitude. This practice shifts the focus from challenges to blessings, fostering a spirit of thankfulness. It resonates with Psalm 106:1 ('Give thanks to the Lord, for he is good; his love endures forever').

Community Prayer Meetings: Establish or participate in regular prayer meetings with fellow Christian educators. Unity in prayer fosters a supportive community and reinforces the concept that 'where two or three gather in my name, there am I with them' (Matthew 18:20).

By weaving these prayers, scriptures, and practices into their daily routine, Christian educators not only navigate professional challenges but also cultivate a resilient and spiritually grounded approach to their calling.

The Concept of Forgiveness

The concept of forgiveness plays a pivotal role in handling perceived animosity from the principal, echoing the profound biblical teachings on forgiveness and reconciliation. One powerful biblical principle that resonates in such situations is found in Matthew 6:14-15 (NIV), where Jesus states, 'For if you forgive other people when they sin against you, your heavenly Father will also forgive you. But if you do not forgive others their sins, your Father will not forgive your sins.'

Consider the story of Joseph in Genesis 50:20 (NIV), where he forgives his brothers who had wronged him, saying, 'You intended to harm me, but

God intended it for good to accomplish what is now being done, the saving of many lives.' This narrative illustrates the transformative power of forgiveness and how God can turn adversity into a greater purpose.

So, when facing challenges with a principal, remember the wisdom of Colossians 3:13 (NIV), 'Bear with each other and forgive one another if any of you has a grievance against someone. Forgive as the Lord forgave you.' In adopting this approach, educators can navigate perceived animosity with a spirit of grace and openness, allowing divine principles to guide their actions.

Fostering a Sense of Unity

Christian educators play a crucial role in fostering a sense of unity and collaboration within the school community, even amidst challenges with the principal. The Christian faith offers a solid foundation for building bridges and resolving conflicts, allowing for a harmonious environment that reflects God's love and grace.

One effective strategy is to prioritize open communication and transparency, drawing inspiration from Ephesians 4:29 (NIV): 'Do not let any unwholesome talk come out of your mouths, but only what is helpful for building others up according to their needs, that it may benefit those who listen.' By engaging in constructive and uplifting conversations, educators can contribute to a positive atmosphere within the school.

Additionally, Galatians 5:22-23 (NIV) emphasizes the fruits of the Spirit, including love, patience, and gentleness. Christian educators can embody these qualities in their interactions, fostering a welcoming and supportive environment. Acts of kindness, understanding, and empathy can bridge gaps and pave the way for resolution.

Moreover, seeking guidance through prayer and relying on the biblical principle of turning the other cheek (Matthew 5:39) can provide Christian educators with the strength and resilience needed to navigate challenges with the principal. This approach not only promotes unity but also reflects the transformative power of faith in overcoming obstacles.

In essence, the Christian faith serves as a guiding force, empowering educators to transcend challenges, build unity, and contribute to a collaborative school community.

Reflecting On the Spiritual Battles
& Taking Action

As we delve into the theme of spiritual warfare, it becomes imperative for Christian teachers to discern the subtle nuances between professional challenges and the spiritual battles that may be at play. The Apostle Paul reminds us in Ephesians 6:12 that 'we do not wrestle against flesh and blood, but against the rulers, against the authorities, against the cosmic powers over this present darkness.

In the field of education, this warfare takes on a unique form, as the very essence of shaping young minds becomes a battleground. Consider the scenario where administrators, knowingly or unknowingly, may act as instruments in a spiritual battle aimed at discouraging good teachers and undermining the divine work taking place in classrooms.

To guard against these spiritual attacks, Christian teachers are called to put on the full armor of God, as outlined in Ephesians 6:13-17. This armor, including the belt of truth, the breastplate of righteousness, the shield of faith, the helmet of salvation, and the sword of the Spirit, equips educators with spiritual resilience in the face of challenges.

Connecting with fellow saints and like-minded colleagues becomes a vital strategy. Sharing experiences, praying together, and uplifting one another can serve as a powerful defense against the spiritual forces at work within the educational realm.

Consider the stories of teachers who, through prayer and unity, have withstood the spiritual attacks aimed at discouraging them. These narratives highlight the importance of recognizing the broader spiritual context in which professional challenges unfold.

In essence, the battlefield in education is not merely about lesson plans and classroom management;

it extends into the spiritual realm. By understanding this reality, Christian teachers can navigate challenges with a heightened awareness of the spiritual warfare surrounding them, relying on the armor of God and the support of their spiritual community.

Notes

_____

_____

_____

_____

_____

_____

_____

_____

_____

_____

_____

_____

_____

_____

A Teacher's Prayer for
"The Principal Don't Like Me"

Heavenly Father,

I come before You seeking Your divine grace and guidance as I navigate the challenges of a situation where there may be misunderstandings. Grant me the strength to maintain a positive and Christ-like attitude in all interactions, especially with my principal. Help me exemplify the qualities of kindness, understanding, and sincerity.

Lord, let Your light shine through me, illuminating my intentions and actions. Assist me in demonstrating that my purpose aligns with the calling You've placed upon my heart. May Your love and grace be evident in my words and deeds.

I humbly ask for Your intervention in the perceptions of my principal. Soften their heart and guide them to see the goodness within me. Grant them discernment to recognize the positive impact I strive to make in the lives of those I teach.

May this situation be an opportunity for growth, understanding, and unity. In Your name, I pray. Amen.

Scriptures When We Need Them the Most

These scriptures emphasize themes of trust, overcoming fear, seeking God's peace, and finding strength in the face of challenges. They can serve as a source of encouragement and resilience for teachers navigating difficult situations, including the perception of not being favored by the principal.

Philippians 4:6-7 (NIV): Do not be anxious about anything, but in every situation, by prayer and petition,

with thanksgiving, present your requests to God. And the peace of God, which transcends all understanding, will guard your hearts and your minds in Christ Jesus.

Psalm 27:1 (NIV): The Lord is my light and my salvation—whom shall, I fear? The Lord is the stronghold of my life—of whom shall I be afraid?

Psalm 34:17-18 (NIV): The righteous cry out, and the Lord hears them; he delivers them from all their troubles. The Lord is close to the brokenhearted and saves those who are crushed in spirit.

Romans 8:31 (NIV): What, then, shall we say in response to these things? If God is for us, who can be against us?

1 Peter 5:7 (NIV): Cast all your anxiety on him because he cares for you.

SECTION THREE

Parents Riding My Back
Faith guiding you with unrealistic parents

My faith has not only been a guiding force but a transformative power when facing parents with seemingly unrealistic expectations for their children's academic performance. Through prayer, I sought divine wisdom and guidance, asking not just for the right words but also for the right spirit to approach these delicate situations.

In these moments, I discovered that the effectiveness of communication is not solely about the content of the message but the manner in which it is delivered. I've learned that the power of 'no' can be softened when accompanied by empathy, understanding, and a tone of genuine concern for the child's well-being.

Consider this parallel with our interactions with God – when we seek something, His response might not always be a direct 'no,' but rather a redirection or spontaneous unfolding of events. This realization has strengthened my faith and conviction, enabling me to navigate challenging conversations with parents with grace and confidence.

In essence, the growth of our faith is directly proportional to our ability to gracefully address the sometimes-unrealistic expectations of parents, turning potential conflicts into opportunities for understanding and collaboration.

Moments of Unwarranted Demands

In moments fraught with unwarranted demands from parents, maintaining a Christ-like attitude becomes not just a choice but a testament to our commitment as Christian teachers. It's an arduous task, requiring a spirit of humility that keeps us grounded and connected with the divine source of our strength.

Embracing humbleness becomes our guiding principle, a virtue that not only defines our character but serves as a bridge to understanding the unique challenges parents may face. Recognizing that parents may not be as equipped with the insights we possess, we are reminded of the importance of patience as a virtue.

Teaching, for me, is not just a profession; it's a ministry. The expectations from the community are immense, mirroring the weight of responsibility that comes with a divine calling. In these moments, I draw parallels between the demands placed on us as teachers and the expectations set for us in ministry, reinforcing the idea that our Christ-like response is not just a reflection of our character but a powerful influence on the dynamics between educators, parents, and the community.

In embracing a Christ-like attitude and responding with grace and patience, we not only navigate challenging situations but transform them into opportunities for empathy, understanding, and ultimately, collaboration.

Applying Biblical Principles

As we navigate the delicate balance between meeting parents' expectations and adhering to educational standards and fairness in grading, it becomes imperative to anchor our approach in timeless biblical principles. Drawing inspiration from scriptures that resonate with the essence of righteousness and fairness, we find a solid foundation on which to stand.

One guiding principle is the assurance that the Holy Spirit is our constant companion, providing wisdom and discernment in moments of decision-making. Trusting in the divine guidance, we can confidently embrace the saying 'peace be still,' recognizing that our commitment to fairness aligns with the higher purpose we serve.

In applying these biblical principles, we not only stand firm in our convictions but also create an environment where fairness and righteousness are not just educational standards but a reflection of our unwavering commitment to the principles of justice. As we navigate this delicate balance, let our actions echo the divine wisdom that guides us, ensuring that our grading practices align with the principles that transcend the earthly realm.

Reflecting on the Theme of Emmanuel

As we traverse the intricate path of teaching, the theme of Emmanuel, 'God with us,' becomes a reassuring melody in our professional journey. In moments of challenging interactions with parents, where the weight of responsibility and expectations may seem overwhelming, we find solace in the unwavering presence of Jesus.

Just as the timeless hymn echoes, 'There's not a friend like the lowly Jesus, no not one, not one,' we are reminded that in our educational walk, we are not alone. Jesus, the truest and most steadfast companion, understands our struggles and is ever-ready to guide us through the complexities of teacher-parent interactions.

In the melodic assurance that 'He knows all about our struggles; He will guide till the day is done,' we find a source of divine guidance that transcends the challenges we encounter. So, let us lean on the comforting truth that Jesus walks beside us, offering wisdom, patience, and grace in every interaction. This acknowledgment transforms each encounter into an opportunity to reflect the divine light that guides our steps in the noble calling of teaching.

Ways We Can Build a Bridge Between Parents

Embarking on the profound journey of education, Christian educators are called not only to teach but to build bridges of understanding and communication with the parents of their students. The pathway to success lies not just in the classroom but in cultivating a deeper knowledge of our students, their families, and the rich cultural tapestry that surrounds us.

As we immerse ourselves in this process of connection, we lay the foundation for a bridge between the fervent desires' parents harbor for their children's success and the nuanced realities of the educational environment. This bridge is built on the pillars of genuine interest, empathy, and cultural sensitivity, ensuring that open lines of communication flourish.

In the tapestry of education, where each thread represents a unique student and family, our commitment to understanding and connecting becomes the loom that weaves a narrative of shared success. This holistic approach transforms the educational experience into a collaborative journey where parents, educators, and students stride together toward the common goal of academic achievement and personal growth."

Don't Forget the Concept of Salvation

The concept of salvation is not just a theological notion but a lifeline for teachers navigating the tumultuous waters of parental demands. In the vast sea of expectations and stress, the idea of salvation becomes a beacon of solace and purpose, offering a transformative perspective to those who feel burdened in their teaching journey.

Imagine a teacher on the brink, overwhelmed by the relentless weight of parents' demands. This burden, if left unaddressed, can lead educators to contemplate leaving the profession they were once called to. Mental health concerns become a shadow, casting a gloom over the passion that once fueled their commitment.

In schools worldwide, the issue of teacher well-being has gained prominence as the recognition of mental, physical, and spiritual health intertwining becomes increasingly evident. The struggle is universal, and educators are reminded to be mindful of these holistic health issues. Yet, in the midst of these challenges, the concept of salvation emerges as a powerful antidote.

I've witnessed colleagues who, in moments of despair, found solace in seeking salvation. The concept of surrendering their burdens to a higher power became a lifeline, a reminder that when all else fails, God remains steadfast. It's a plea for divine intervention in the intricate tapestry of their lives.

The burdens we carry as teachers can be overwhelming, threatening to extinguish the flame of our calling. Yet, in the concept of salvation, we discover a profound truth – an invitation to include God in our struggles. It's a recognition that, even when the road seems arduous, the burden lightens when shared with a higher power.

This concept becomes everything – a refuge for the weary, a balm for the wounded, and a source of strength for those on the verge of giving up. Salvation, when sought and embraced, transforms the narrative of despair into one of hope and endurance.

Let us not forget that when God bestows something upon us, it is always good, irrespective of how it may appear or seem. The concept of salvation becomes a lifeline that teachers can grasp, not just as a theological abstraction, but as a tangible reality in their journey of resilience and purpose.

Faith Played a Role in Overcoming
Challenges with Parents

Facing challenges with parents can be emotionally taxing, especially when influenced by colleagues. I distinctly recall a situation where my colleagues seemingly orchestrated a conflict with a parent regarding services provided to their child. The atmosphere was charged with anxiety, and I felt the weight of isolation.

In those moments of despair, I turned to my faith. Recognizing that I was a child of God, I fervently prayed for divine intervention. The Holy Spirit became my advocate, and I sought support from above. The transformation was remarkable; what was once a sense of helplessness evolved into a feeling of divine coverage.

Before I asked for divine help, I navigated the situation alone, overwhelmed by the looming conflict. However, with my faith as my anchor, I pressed on with calm determination. I knew my intentions were pure, and I believed that God had my back.

Asking the Holy Spirit to step in and take control was a turning point. The challenges that once seemed insurmountable gradually shifted toward a positive outcome. It reinforced a truth that I hold dear – when you invite God into your challenges, positive results follow.

This experience solidified my conviction that no matter the influence or complexity, faith is the ultimate ally in overcoming challenges with parents. Trusting in God's guidance not only changed the course of that specific situation but also strengthened my resolve to face future challenges with unwavering faith.

Notes

_____

_____

_____

_____

_____

_____

_____

_____

_____

_____

_____

A Teacher's Prayer for Parents Riding My Back

Heavenly Father,

I approach Your throne seeking Your wisdom and divine intervention as I face challenges with parents. Grant me the strength to navigate these situations with grace, understanding, and a Christ-centered heart.

Lord, I desire to foster an environment of peace and harmony between myself and the parents of my students. Help me to communicate effectively, to build bridges of understanding, and to create a partnership for the benefit of the children entrusted to my care.

I yearn to teach with integrity, holding students accountable for their learning based on fair assessments. Grant me the courage to uphold educational standards and resist external pressures that may compromise the integrity of the educational process.

Lord, I place these concerns at Your feet, trusting in Your guidance to bring resolution and peace. May Your wisdom be my guide as I strive to fulfill my teaching responsibilities with excellence. In Your name, I pray. Amen.

Scriptures When We Need Them the Most

When dealing with parents and their expectations, these scriptures provide a foundation for relying on faith, seeking God's wisdom, and approaching situations with grace and love. Teachers can use these verses as sources of inspiration and reflection during challenging moments.

Philippians 4:6-7 (NIV): "Do not be anxious about anything, but in every situation, by prayer and petition, with thanksgiving, present your requests to God. And the peace of God, which transcends all understanding, will guard your hearts and your minds in Christ Jesus."

This scripture encourages teachers to turn to prayer in moments of anxiety or stress, seeking God's guidance and peace.

Proverbs 3:5-6 (NIV): "Trust in the Lord with all your heart and lean not on your own understanding; in all your ways submit to him, and he will make your paths straight.

Teachers can find comfort in trusting God's guidance and submitting challenging situations to Him.

Colossians 3:23 (NIV): "Whatever you do, work at it with all your heart, as working for the Lord, not for human masters."

This scripture can serve as a reminder for teachers to focus on their work with dedication and integrity, regardless of external pressures.

James 1:5 (NIV): "If any of you lacks wisdom, you should ask God, who gives generously to all without finding fault, and it will be given to you."

Seeking wisdom through prayer is emphasized in this scripture, which can be applicable when teachers need guidance in handling difficult conversations.

Ephesians 4:2-3 (NIV): "Be completely humble and gentle; be patient, bearing one another in love. Make every effort to keep the unity of the Spirit through the bond of peace."

This scripture encourages teachers to approach conflicts with humility, gentleness, and patience, fostering unity and peace.

Section 4

Too Many Meeting/Too Many Demands

Picture this: it's the end of a long day of teaching, and now, instead of heading home, it's time to gather for yet another faculty meeting. We've all been there, and if you're a teacher, you know the struggle. These meetings, while sometimes beneficial, can often feel like an extra layer of exhaustion piled on an already demanding profession.

In the realm of education, where every minute is precious, the incessant demand for meetings can quickly lead to burnout. The teaching profession, noble as it is, comes with its fair share of challenges, and the constant stream of meetings is one of them. It begs the question – are all these meetings truly necessary?

As educators, we understand the importance of collaboration and communication. However, what if there was a more efficient way? In this chapter, I delve into the impact of unnecessary meetings on teachers, exploring the challenges they bring, and proposing a more thoughtful approach.

I believe administrators could play a pivotal role in alleviating this burden. Imagine if there was a strategic plan, distinguishing essential in-person meetings from those that could be virtual or even watched at a later time. It's about trusting teachers to manage their time effectively, without compromising the essence of collaboration.

Even as Christian teachers, we're not immune to the toll of these meetings. Join me in navigating the landscape of unnecessary meetings, discovering how a more mindful approach can not only save time but also preserve the passion and purpose that brought us into this noble profession.

Work-Life Balance and Overall Well-Being

Frequent and unnecessary meetings don't just disrupt a Christian teacher's work-life balance; they become a relentless assault on their mental, emotional, and spiritual well-being. Picture this: the day of the meeting dawns, and what should be an opportunity for collaboration feels more like a looming challenge, turning an ordinary day into an arduous journey.

Mentally, it transforms the day into a marathon before the first bell even rings. The mental toll is palpable as a teacher navigates through what becomes an unexpectedly lengthy day. It's in these moments that the power of prayer becomes a lifeline, a plea for strength and endurance to overcome the mental challenges.

Emotionally, the effects are like a storm passing through. Irritability and a short temper become unwelcome companions, threatening to overshadow the teacher's usual dedication to school activities, curriculum, and meaningful connections with students. The emotional toll is real, and it takes a conscious effort to stay connected and invested.

Spiritually, the impact is profound. The exhaustion from unnecessary meetings may extend beyond the school gates, making it challenging to attend midweek church services or participate in Bible study. The spiritual fuel that sustains us is depleted, and finding the energy to recharge becomes an uphill battle.

In essence, these meetings aren't just time-consuming; they are energy-draining events that test the resilience of a Christian teacher's mind, heart, and spirit. Navigating through such challenges requires not just professional fortitude but a deep reliance on faith to overcome the toll these meetings exact on every level.

Constant Demands Disrupt a
Christian Teacher's Ability

Constant demands, especially in the form of excessive meetings, cast a pervasive shadow over a Christian teacher's calling and sense of purpose in their noble profession. Imagine this: the relentless demands not only drain the teacher's energy but also cast a veil over the positive contributions they make. It's a scenario where the good often gets overshadowed by the negative.

Consider a teacher who, due to the overwhelming demands of constant meetings, occasionally misses faculty and staff gatherings. The impact is not just on attendance; it ripples through faculty morale, creating an environment where the positive efforts of the teacher seem minimal. It's a subtle but potent erosion of the sense of purpose and fulfillment that should accompany the teaching profession.

Moreover, when the demands become excessive, it can force teachers to resort to measures like taking a day off on meeting days, hoping to escape the prolonged hours. Yet, this very act unintentionally amplifies the challenges, making it seem like a struggle to endure the demands rather than relishing the opportunity to educate and nurture students.

In essence, these constant demands disrupt the harmony between a teacher's calling and their ability to find purpose in their profession. It's not just about attending meetings; it's about how these demands shape the narrative of a teacher's commitment, dedication, and impact on the lives of their students.

Christian Teachers Can
Maintain Their Faith

In the relentless storm of too many meetings and demands, Christian teachers can discover a sanctuary within their faith, finding resilience and strength amidst the chaos. It's not just about surviving; it's about thriving in the face of burnout.

One powerful strategy is fostering connections with fellow teachers who share the same faith. These connections can become pillars of support, uplifting each other during challenging times. Imagine the strength that comes from a community that shares not only the professional challenges but also the spiritual journey.

Consistent prayer becomes not just a routine but a lifeline. Picture a Christian teacher taking a moment before and after each demanding meeting, seeking divine guidance and finding solace in the midst of chaos. It's in these moments of prayer that resilience is built, and faith becomes an anchor, keeping the teacher grounded and centered.

Consider the impact of incorporating daily devotion into the routine. Reading scriptures that resonate with the challenges faced, accompanied by reflections and prayers, can provide a daily dose of inspiration and a reminder of the higher purpose behind the profession.

In essence, it's not just about staying connected to faith; it's about leveraging that connection as a transformative force. Christian teachers can not only endure burnout but emerge from it with strengthened faith, ready to navigate the demanding landscape with grace and purpose.

Biblical Principles or Scriptures That Can Offer Guidance

In the labyrinth of burnout caused by excessive meetings, Christian teachers can turn to timeless biblical principles and scriptures for more than just solace – they can find a roadmap to rejuvenation and renewed purpose.

Consider the comforting words of Psalms 23, reminding teachers that even in the busiest valleys, God is their shepherd, guiding them with divine wisdom and providing the rest they need. Reflecting on this passage during moments of exhaustion can transform weariness into a sense of being cared for and protected.

Another source of guidance could be Philippians 4:6-7, encouraging teachers not to be anxious but to bring their concerns to God in prayer. Picture a Christian teacher taking a moment before each overwhelming meeting, centering themselves in prayer, and finding peace that surpasses understanding.

Proverbs 3:5-6 offers a timeless principle – trusting in the Lord with all your heart and leaning not on your own understanding. Applying this to the challenges of excessive meetings can foster a sense of surrender, reminding teachers that they don't have to carry the burden alone.

By delving into these biblical principles and scriptures, Christian teachers can not only find solace but also uncover a wellspring of wisdom and strength. It's not just about weathering the storm; it's about emerging from it with renewed faith and resilience.

School Leaders Can Support Christian Teachers

As Christian teachers navigate the delicate balance between professional demands and faith commitments, administrators hold a key role in shaping an environment that nurtures both. Instead of merely acknowledging the challenge, administrators can actively champion solutions and implement supportive measures.

Consider the possibility of introducing a flexible meeting schedule, allowing teachers to attend in person, virtually, or view recordings later. This not only respects their time but also acknowledges their commitment to both the school and their faith.

Administrators can also explore streamlined communication channels, ensuring that essential information is conveyed efficiently, reducing the need for excessive meetings. By leveraging technology and strategic planning, the administrative team can foster an atmosphere of collaboration without overburdening teachers.

Moreover, administrators might consider incorporating moments of spiritual reflection or prayer into the school day, providing Christian teachers with a brief respite to recharge and find strength in their faith.

These proactive measures not only demonstrate an understanding of the unique challenges faced by Christian teachers but also contribute to a more supportive and harmonious school culture. In essence, administrators have the power to shape an environment where teachers can thrive both professionally and spiritually.

Notes

_____

_____

_____

_____

_____

_____

_____

_____

_____

_____

_____

_____

_____

_____

_____

_____

_____

A Teacher's Prayer for Too Many Meetings/Too
Many Demands

Heavenly Father,

I come before You, seeking Your divine presence
and strength as I grapple with the challenges of too
many meetings and excessive demands. Grant me the
patience to navigate through these situations with a
calm and steadfast spirit.

Lord, in the midst of overwhelming demands, help
me find moments of tranquility and focus. Provide me

with the resilience to endure, the discernment to prioritize, and the wisdom to manage my time effectively.

May Your peace, which surpasses all understanding, guard my heart and mind in the midst of busyness. Empower me to approach each meeting and demand with a spirit of grace and purpose.

I surrender these burdens to You, trusting in Your guidance to navigate this season with patience and resilience. In Your name, I pray. Amen.

Scriptures when we need them the most

Philippians 4:6-7 (NIV): "Do not be anxious about anything, but in every situation, by prayer and petition, with thanksgiving, present your requests to God. And the peace of God, which transcends all understanding, will guard your hearts and your minds in Christ Jesus.

Matthew 11:28-30 (NIV): "Come to me, all you who are weary and burdened, and I will give you rest. Take my yoke upon you and learn from me, for I am gentle and humble in heart, and you will find rest for your souls. For my yoke is easy, and my burden is light."

Isaiah 40:31 (NIV): "But those who hope in the Lord will renew their strength. They will soar on wings like eagles; they will run and not grow weary, they will walk and not be faint."

Proverbs 3:5-6 (NIV): "Trust in the Lord with all your heart and lean not on your own understanding; in all your ways submit to him, and he will make your paths straight."

Psalm 23:1-3 (NIV): "The Lord is my shepherd, I lack nothing. He makes me lie down in green pastures, he leads me beside quiet waters, he refreshes my soul."

James 1:5 (NIV): "If any of you lacks wisdom, you should ask God, who gives generously to all without finding fault, and it will be given to you."

Section 5

Where's Salvation When You Need It?

Salvation is something that we can't buy, sell or give it to someone. No one can get it for you and wrap it up in a gift and give it to you. "Imagine standing at the crossroads of burnout, exhaustion, and the relentless demands of the teaching profession. In the midst of this chaos, the concept of salvation beckons. But where is it when we need it the most? Salvation, a divine gift we can't trade or purchase, is intricately woven into the fabric of our lives.

Picture this journey as a quest for utopia, a sanctuary from the overwhelming challenges that threaten our sanity. Section 5 invites us to explore the 'how,' 'why,' and 'what' of maintaining salvation amid the chaos of burnout. It's not just about seeking solace; it's about understanding the role of the Holy Spirit, the choices we make, and the people we surround ourselves with.

The Concept of Salvation

The concept of salvation plays a vital role in the life of a Christian teacher grappling with burnout and exhaustion in the teaching profession. Let me share a powerful example that illustrates the profound impact of salvation in such challenging times.

Consider the story of Sarah, an experienced teacher on the verge of burnout. Overwhelmed by the incessant demands of her job, she felt mentally, emotionally, and spiritually drained. In the midst of this turmoil, Sarah turned to her faith, seeking salvation as a refuge. Through fervent prayer and meditation on specific scriptures that resonated with her struggles, she experienced a transformative journey.

One particular biblical passage, Psalm 23:1-3, became her anchor: 'The Lord is my shepherd; I shall not want. He makes me lie down in green pastures. He leads me beside still waters. He restores my soul.' This verse became a source of comfort and strength, guiding Sarah through the tumultuous sea of burnout.

In embracing salvation, Sarah found solace not only in the words of the scripture but also in the support of her fellow Christian teachers. They formed a prayer group, lifting each other up during challenging times and collectively seeking guidance from the Holy Spirit.

This example illustrates how the concept of salvation is not just a theoretical notion but a practical and transformative force. It showcases the real-life impact of faith, providing the strength needed to endure burnout and emerge with a renewed sense of purpose.

Inability To Buy or Sell Salvation

The inability to buy or sell salvation elevates it to a status of unparalleled uniqueness and priceless significance. Imagine it as a rare and exquisite treasure, hidden in the depths of our spiritual journey, accessible only to those who embark on the quest of seeking God's divine intervention.

Salvation is intangible, elusive to the eye, yet its presence is profoundly felt in the depths of our hearts. It's not a transaction with a tangible price tag; instead, it's a transcendent experience that transforms the very fabric of our being. Picture salvation as a radiant light that emanates from within, illuminating not just our own path but also touching the lives of those around us.

This priceless gift is beyond the constraints of commerce, reminding us that its value is immeasurable. It's a spiritual currency that cannot be bought or sold, emphasizing that salvation is not subject to the whims of market forces or external influences. In this context, the inability to buy or sell salvation serves as a powerful reminder that its acquisition is a sacred and personal journey, a divine exchange between the seeker and the Creator.

Salvation, in its uniqueness, becomes a beacon of hope, a source of strength that defies the limitations of material wealth. It is the ultimate gift, bestowed upon those who humbly seek, and its priceless nature resonates in the transformative impact it has on our lives and the lives of those we touch.

In Quest for Utopia

In the pursuit of utopia, every teacher envisions a perfect haven, a sanctuary untouched by the chaos of the world. However, in the noble quest to maintain spiritual well-being amid the relentless demands of our profession, we encounter challenges that test the very essence of our faith.

Picture this journey as a daring expedition into uncharted territories, where the landscape is dotted with trials and tribulations. The challenges, like unpredictable storms, can shake the foundations of our strength in the Lord and challenge the core of our beliefs. It's a package deal, an inevitable part of the teacher's sojourn, akin to the trials that accompany the declaration of love for the Lord.

Navigating these challenges requires preparation, much like gearing up for battle. We must fortify our spiritual armor and brace ourselves for the unexpected. The demands of the teaching profession, like fierce adversaries, may attempt to cast shadows on our spiritual path. Yet, it's precisely within these challenges that our faith is sculpted and strengthened.

As we march through the trials, let us not forget that utopia is not the absence of challenges but the triumph over them. The journey toward spiritual well-being in the teaching profession is not a linear path but a courageous exploration into the heart of our beliefs, where each challenge becomes a steppingstone toward the utopia we seek—the perfect alignment of our profession and our spiritual journey.

Understanding The Holy Spirit

Unlocking the depths of salvation and finding resilience in the face of burnout requires an intimate understanding of the Holy Spirit—an ethereal force that serves as our divine connection to God. Picture the Holy Spirit as the guiding light, the celestial bridge that links believers to the very essence of salvation.

In the intricate tapestry of faith, the Holy Spirit plays a pivotal role as the revealer of God's thoughts. It's the compass that directs believers through the labyrinth of challenges, unveiling profound truths along the way.

Much like a celestial guide, the Holy Spirit is our constant companion, navigating us through the tumultuous seas of burnout.

Consider the Holy Spirit as the whisperer of solace in moments of exhaustion, the gentle force that breathes life into our weary spirits.

It's not merely an abstract concept but a tangible manifestation of God's grace, a spiritual compass that points us towards the path of salvation and resilience.

To truly grasp the importance of the Holy Spirit, let's delve into real-life stories of believers who, amidst the storms of burnout, found solace and strength through their connection to the divine.

These narratives illuminate the transformative power of the Holy Spirit, showcasing its ability to guide believers through the darkest nights and lead them towards the dawn of spiritual rejuvenation.

In essence, the understanding of the Holy Spirit transcends theological principles; it becomes a lived experience—a journey that intertwines our salvation and resilience with the ethereal presence of the divine."

Choices to Nurture and Preserve

In the intricate dance of professional life, a Christian teacher holds the power to shape their journey and actively preserve their salvation. One pivotal choice involves selecting the right school, church, and community—a trinity of influences that can either fortify or challenge their faith.

Imagine choosing a school where the ethos aligns seamlessly with your spiritual values—a place where the very atmosphere fosters a sense of divine connection. The right school becomes a sanctuary, a space where the complexities of professional life are met with a harmonious blend of faith and purpose.

Similarly, the choice of a church adds another layer to the tapestry of salvation. It's not merely a physical place of worship but a spiritual anchor—a community of believers who uplift, inspire, and share in the trials and triumphs of a Christian teacher's journey. Consider the spiritual resilience that blossoms within a congregation that echoes the teacher's commitment to faith.

Beyond the school and church, the choice of community completes the triad. A supportive community becomes fertile soil where the seeds of salvation can flourish, providing the necessary nutrients to weather the storms of professional complexities. It's a network of like-minded individuals who share the same commitment to faith and understand the unique challenges faced by a Christian teacher.

However, let's acknowledge the reality that even in the most carefully chosen environments, trials and tribulations may emerge. It's a testament to the profound truth that salvation isn't a shield against challenges but a guiding force that illuminates the path forward. The choices we make actively nurture and preserve our salvation, transforming the complexities of professional life into opportunities for spiritual growth and resilience.

Surrounding Ourselves with Influence

The profound impact of salvation is intricately tied to the people we choose to surround ourselves with on this journey. Imagine these individuals as co-travelers, each influencing the tenor of our salvation experience. In this intricate dance, negative companions can cast shadows, while those who share our faith become radiant beacons of support.

Consider the scenario where negativity permeates the atmosphere. The presence of individuals who lack a God-fearing spirit may breed misunderstanding and a lack of empathy for our salvation walk. These nonaligned companions, unknowingly or knowingly, can cast doubt on the sanctity of our journey.

However, the transformative power of salvation lies not just in recognizing the potential pitfalls but in proactively shaping the environment. As teachers navigating the complexities of professional life, we hold the reins to curate a supportive and spiritually uplifting community.

One strategy involves intentionally seeking out and fostering connections with like-minded individuals who share our commitment to faith. These connections become pillars of strength, providing empathy, understanding, and shared experiences on the path of salvation. It's a conscious effort to build a community that aligns with our spiritual values.

Additionally, the power of influence works both ways. As teachers, we possess the agency to infuse positivity and God-fearing values into our immediate circles. By radiating the light of our faith, we contribute to the creation of an uplifting environment, where the collective journey towards salvation becomes a shared and enriching experience.

In essence, salvation is not a solitary endeavor but a communal voyage. The people we surround ourselves with play a pivotal role in shaping the narrative of our salvation experience. By employing strategies to foster a supportive and spiritually uplifting environment, teachers can navigate the challenges of professional life with resilience, surrounded by a community that echoes the divine purpose of their journey.

Salvation Serving as a Guiding Light

The concept of salvation emerges as a radiant beacon, a guiding light that illuminates the path for Christian teachers seeking solace and purpose amidst the tumult of overwhelming challenges. In the tapestry of this divine journey, there are multifaceted ways through which salvation becomes a source of unwavering guidance.

Imagine the teacher, standing at the crossroads of fatigue, frustration, and the ceaseless demands of the profession. In this crucible of challenges, salvation isn't a distant concept but an immediate and tangible source of strength. It serves as a compass, pointing towards solace and purpose, urging teachers to anchor themselves in their faith.

One significant way salvation guides teachers is by fostering a continual connection with God. Through prayer, reflection, and a conscious effort to maintain spiritual communion, teachers can draw from the wellspring of divine wisdom and resilience. It's not just a theoretical belief but a practical reality – the act of seeking solace in God's presence becomes an active, guiding force.

Moreover, the concept of salvation shapes the teacher's choices in companionship. By surrounding themselves with kindred spirits who share their faith, teachers create a supportive community that reinforces the guiding light of salvation. The shared belief becomes a collective source of encouragement, fostering an environment where purpose is sustained.

Salvation also plays a pivotal role in reframing challenges as opportunities for growth. Rather than viewing obstacles as insurmountable barriers, teachers, anchored in the concept of salvation, can perceive them as transformative moments. The journey towards solace and purpose becomes a dynamic process of learning, adapting, and relying on the divine guidance embedded in salvation.

In essence, salvation isn't an abstract ideal but a guiding light with practical implications for the lives of

Christian teachers. It weaves through the fabric of their experiences, offering not just solace but a profound sense of purpose. As teachers navigate the overwhelming challenges, salvation stands as a constant companion, illuminating the way forward with the brilliance of divine light."

Considering Salvation a Sanctuary

Salvation, a precious gift attained through our acceptance of Jesus as our Lord and Savior, transforms into more than a concept—it becomes a sanctuary, a refuge that resides in the very core of our being. Picture it as a sacred haven, not just a distant hope but a tangible reality etched into our hearts and minds.

In the chaos of life, when exhaustion and storms threaten to overwhelm us, salvation stands as an unwavering sanctuary. It's not merely a peace we hope for; it's a peace we carry within us. This sanctuary isn't confined to the four walls of a church; it unfolds in the way we navigate our daily existence.

Consider the way salvation permeates our actions and interactions. It shapes the way we speak, the way we teach, and the way we engage with others. It becomes the calming force in the midst of life's storms, providing a sanctuary not just for ourselves but for those around us.

Visualize a teacher, weary from the demands of the profession, finding solace in the sanctuary of salvation. It's not an abstract ideal but a tangible source of strength. It influences the demeanor with which they face challenges, offering a refuge that goes beyond the surface. This sanctuary empowers the teacher to stay calm, composed, and steadfast, even in the most tumultuous moments.

In the sanctuary of salvation, we discover not just a theoretical peace but a transformative power. It becomes a sanctuary that goes beyond individual moments of chaos—it's a constant presence, a refuge we carry within, ready to provide strength and solace whenever needed. As we navigate the complexities of life, salvation stands as a sanctuary, a sacred space that shapes our existence and offers refuge amid the storms.

Lessons Drawn from Salvation

Every day unfolds a new chapter in the intricate tapestry of our lives, woven seamlessly with the threads of salvation, especially within the context of a teacher's journey. It's a narrative where each moment, each interaction, and each challenge hold valuable lessons waiting to be discovered.

In my own journey spanning 30 plus years, I've encountered numerous friends, each contributing a unique thread to the fabric of my life. Every day, I find myself learning something new about them, and through these connections, I've gleaned profound insights into the essence of salvation's intertwining with our existence.

There have been instances where friends promised to make my life easier, only to fall short of those promises. Yet, amidst these human inconsistencies, my unwavering faith and trust in God have allowed me to experience a profound sense of comfort. It's a rule deeply embedded in the fabric of our spiritual journey—humans may let us down every day, but God, the steadfast presence, will never leave nor forsake us. This is not just a belief; it's a truth that resonates in the very fibers of our being.

Consider the daily lessons emerging from this interplay of salvation with life's intricate fabric. It's a constant reminder that our journey, much like a tapestry, is rich with diversity, unpredictability, and, most importantly, divine guidance. The threads of salvation weave through the challenges, the victories, and the ordinary moments, offering profound insights into the nature of trust, faith, and the unwavering support that comes from above.

As a teacher navigating the complexities of the profession, these lessons become a guiding light. The intertwining of salvation with our journey isn't just a theoretical concept; it's a living reality that shapes our responses, our resilience, and our ability to find meaning in every chapter of the unfolding story. In the classroom, amidst the demands of education, and in personal connections, these lessons offer a profound perspective—a tapestry of life intricately woven with the divine threads of salvation, beckoning us to find meaning, purpose, and unwavering strength in the embrace of our faith."

The 'How,' 'Why,' and 'What' of Maintaining Salvation

As teachers, delving into the intricacies of the 'how,' 'why,' and 'what' of maintaining salvation becomes a profound journey of self-discovery. It's a roadmap guiding us through the labyrinth of our experiences, unraveling the mysteries of our spiritual resilience and well-being, particularly in the face of burnout.

Understanding the 'how' invites us to introspect, to grasp the mechanisms that propel us forward or pull us into the depths of exhaustion. It's a conscious exploration of the choices we make, the moments of solace we seek, and the daily practices that either fortify or compromise our salvation. It's about deciphering the intricate dance between our actions and the divine grace that sustains us.

The 'why' introduces a reflective lens to our journey. Why do certain challenges manifest in our lives, especially when they seem overwhelming? Why do we navigate burnout, and to what extent do we permit our salvation to be a guiding force? Unraveling these 'whys' isn't merely a philosophical exercise; it's a profound inquiry into the purpose behind our struggles, offering insights that can redefine our responses to adversity.

Then comes the 'what'—the pivotal question of what degree we allow our salvation to be compromised. It's a call to accountability, urging us to assess our boundaries, our faith, and our commitment to preserving the sanctity of our spiritual well-being. The 'what' invites us to draw a line in the sand, a line that burnout cannot cross, safeguarded by the unwavering strength of our salvation.

As we navigate this journey of exploration, the impact on our resilience and spiritual well-being becomes tangible. The 'how,' 'why,' and 'what' aren't mere intellectual exercises; they are tools that empower us. They empower us to comprehend our situations with clarity, to cultivate resilience in the face of burnout, and to nurture our spiritual well-being as an anchor in the storm.

In the classroom, where challenges are diverse and demanding, this understanding becomes a source of strength. It transforms burnout from an inevitable threat to a surmountable challenge, and our salvation emerges not just as a concept but as a living force guiding us toward resilience, purpose, and enduring spiritual well-being.

Notes

_____

_____

_____

_____

_____

_____

_____

_____

_____

_____

_____

_____

_____

_____

_____

_____

_____

_____

_____

A Teacher's Prayer for Salvation

Heavenly Father, in the midst of the chaos and demands of the teaching profession, I come to You seeking the divine gift of salvation. I acknowledge that this gift cannot be bought or traded but is freely given by Your grace.

Lord, I find myself at the crossroads of burnout and exhaustion, and I need Your saving grace to guide me through. Please wrap me in Your love and provide the strength and resilience I need to face the challenges before me.

I surrender my burdens, anxieties, and exhaustion to You, Lord. May Your peace, which surpasses all understanding, fill my heart and soul. Let this chapter be a turning point, a moment of divine intervention in my life.

I believe and trust that, through this prayer, I will find the salvation I need. In Jesus' name, I pray. Amen."

Scriptures When We Need Them The Most

Psalm 34:17-18 (NIV): "The righteous cry out, and the Lord hears them; he delivers them from all their troubles. The Lord is close to the brokenhearted and saves those who are crushed in spirit."

Matthew 11:28-30 (NIV): "Come to me, all you who are weary and burdened, and I will give you rest. Take my yoke upon you and learn from me, for I am gentle and humble in heart, and you will find rest for your souls."

Philippians 4:6-7 (NIV): "Do not be anxious about anything, but in every situation, by prayer and petition, with thanksgiving, present your requests to God. And the peace of God, which transcends all understanding, will guard your hearts and your minds in Christ Jesus."

Isaiah 40:31 (NIV): "But those who hope in the Lord will renew their strength. They will soar on wings like eagles; they will run and not grow weary, they will walk and not be faint."

Jeremiah 29:11 (NIV): "For I know the plans I have for you, declares the Lord, plans for welfare and not for evil, to give you a future and a hope."

Psalm 51:10 (NIV): "Create in me a pure heart, O God, and renew a steadfast spirit within me."

These scriptures can offer comfort, reassurance, and a sense of God's presence during challenging times, contributing to the theme of seeking salvation in the face of burnout and exhaustion.

To My Fellow Christian teachers:

I trust that, guided by the Holy Spirit, I have unraveled the threads of stress and uncertainty, presenting not just a narrative but tangible strategies to navigate the storm. As the curtains opened, I hope you glimpsed the spiritual battles that often disguise themselves as mere professional challenges, reminding us that our true adversaries are not always flesh and blood but spiritual forces in high places.

For those who haven't yet discovered that salvation is the key, I strongly recommend seeking a church home. If you're already a member and haven't experienced salvation, consider meeting with your ministerial staff or exploring a new Christian experience by finding a new church home. Salvation is the word!

As you know, we opened the book within the spirit of 'O Come, O Come, Emmanuel,' and now it's time to close it giving God all the glory. And...may we remember to open our hearts to the Emmanuel who walks with us through the hallways of our profession, offering guidance, solace, and joy. Until next time my friends!

About the Author

Dr. Anthony Dayse is a highly seasoned public-school educator, devoting his life to the transformative power of teaching and inspiration. He has taught in 6 different states. His fervor for education is seamlessly woven with his deep-rooted love for the Lord, shaping both his professional endeavors and written works.

Bringing over three decades of experience as a K-12 public-school teacher, College Instructor and mentor, Dr. Dayse has emerged as a compelling advocate, uplifting educators worldwide.

As an ordained minister, holding a doctorate in Christian Counseling and a master's in education, he possesses a profound comprehension of the subject matter, enabling him to articulate intricate ideas with clarity and precision.

Through his written contributions, Dr. Dayse shares rich insights, personal experiences, and pragmatic advice, aiming to empower teachers at every level and encouraging them to discover joy and purpose in their vocation.

www.ingramcontent.com/pod-product-compliance
Lightning Source LLC
Chambersburg PA
CBHW071012120626
46546CB00003B/1048